*Rosmarie —
Here is how!
Dana*

The
Castle Gargoyle

A Hollyweird Memoir

DANA GRAE KANE

InspiringVoices®
A Service of **Guideposts**

The Castle Gargoyle
Copyright © 2006, 2014 Dana Grae Kane.

Odd Jobs
Copyright © 2014 Dana Grae Kane.

All rights reserved. No part of this book may be used or reproduced by any means, graphic, electronic, or mechanical, including photocopying, recording, taping or by any information storage retrieval system without the written permission of the publisher except in the case of brief quotations embodied in critical articles and reviews.

Inspiring Voices books may be ordered through booksellers or by contacting:

Inspiring Voices
1663 Liberty Drive
Bloomington, IN 47403
www.inspiringvoices.com
1 (866) 697-5313

Gargoyle Cover graphic with permission © 2006 David Harriman
Interior gargoyle graphic courtesy labamba @ CanStockPhoto.com
Odd Jobs art with permission © 2013 Charlotte Creel

Because of the dynamic nature of the Internet, any web addresses or links contained in this book may have changed since publication and may no longer be valid. The views expressed in this work are solely those of the author and do not necessarily reflect the views of the publisher, and the publisher hereby disclaims any responsibility for them.

Any people depicted in stock imagery provided by Thinkstock are models, and such images are being used for illustrative purposes only. Certain stock imagery © Thinkstock.

ISBN: 978-1-4624-0898-6 (sc)
ISBN: 978-1-4624-0899-3 (e)

Library of Congress Control Number: 2014901567

Printed in the United States of America.

Inspiring Voices rev. date: 02/05/2104

In memory of my beloved husband, Jay Paul Kane (1926-2007). He saved my life and the lives of countless others.

My husband may be known to many of you for his three inspiring gospel albums, "I Believe in Miracles," "I know Who Holds My Hand" and "Brother Paul Sings Sings Sings for Everyman." Funds from these albums supported struggling congregations of many faiths and denominations.

Born into a traditional Russian Jewish refugee family, he was blessed with an epiphany in his early 20s. Caught in a deadly snow storm without food, shelter or warm clothing, his Savior appeared to him and led him to safety. Ever after, my husband used his magnificent God-given voice to help others find their spiritual path. While the accolades he received for his charity were many, the most meaningful to him were the letters from people he uplifted. The letters often read: "Your voice got me through the night. You saved my life."

Tragically, by 1966 my husband's physical and mental conditions, stemming from severe injuries sustained in two wars and an undetectable brain tumor, made it impossible for him to continue to perform or record. While he was not by then fully cognizant of the honor, in 1967 my husband was elected to the American Society of Composers Authors and Publishers. I determined to do whatever it took to save his life. These memoirs, The Castle Gargoyle and Odd Jobs together tell the story.

Contents

THE CASTLE GARGOYLE

Death and Resurrection 1

The Minor Mobster. 3

The Glory That Was Home 6

Fantasy Furnishings 9

The Secret of the Dusty Desk 13

The Night of the Gilded Guests. 16

St. Francis of Argyle 20

The Art Mart on the Pyre of Fire. 23

Escape from the Dungeon. 27

Epilogue 2013. 29

Odd Jobs

Motivations 39
Counter Attack 42
The Bank Job 47
The Pizza House Bar Grill and Family Restaurant 51
Life or Death. 55
Metamorphosis 58
"Coffee" Chief 1.0. 64
Copy Chief 2.1 69
Copy Chief 2.2 71
The Ironic Health Insurance Company Job. 75
Foreign Affairs Factotum 78
Networking Nets a Great Job 84
Midnight Mail Madness 88
What Now?. 95

Death and Resurrection

THE CASTLE ARGYLE, a beautifully restored 1926 apartment building, graces the corner of Argyle and Palm Streets in Hollywood, California. The cooperative effort of Southern California Presbyterian Homes and the Department of Housing and Urban Development has turned what had degenerated into a tenement into a superb senior residential facility with luxurious appointments and official historic status.

In its first incarnation, the elegant Argyle housed Hollywood luminaries in town for filming, including among many Clark Gable and Cecil B. DeMille. Over time the Castle fell from grace and its spacious suites were divided into smaller apartments. By the 1960s the Dark Ages had descended on the Argyle. It had become home to impoverished actors, petty thieves, junkies, drunks, prostitutes, starving artists, wanna-be rock stars, my husband, JP, and me.

In the tragi-comedy of life, catastrophic medical misfortune brought us to the Castle. An undetectable brain tumor and the health insurance industry did their best to kill my husband and successfully murdered our recording company, then located in the famous Crossroads of the World. Our neighbors there were Mel and Noel Blanc, Lou Rawls, Doris Day, native American screenwriter Robert Bice and cowboy film star Lash LaRue.

The physical and mental horrors my husband suffered and our resulting financial position made our time at the Argyle very difficult; Arthur Rimbaud's <u>A Season in Hell</u> comes to mind. However, the experience also provided some of the most bizarre, humorous and memorable incidents of our lives.

Every word of this tale is true, to the best of my memory. Upon reading this memoir, our dear friend, Jane Lehner, exclaimed: "The Castle Argyle??!! This sounds more like The Castle Gargoyle!!" So it was.

The Minor Mobster

My husband's remarkable musical talent, business acumen, determination and very hard work had taken him from the bottom of the ghetto to the top of the performing and recording arts. In 1967 he was elected to the American Society of Composers, Authors and Publishers, open only to those whose musical works sell in the millions. Highly charitable, he gave most of this away to all manner of medical, civic, religious and academic organizations, never dreaming he could not continue to generate a high income.

The hidden tumor was steadily digging into his brain, undermining his mental and his physical functions to the degree that our business failed. Now deeply mired in debt, we prepared to give up our office and move to the only place we could afford, The Castle Argyle.

While packing up, we had an unexpected visitor. A megalithic recording empire seeking clean independent producers through whom to launder dirty money had presumed we would be desperate enough to sell our souls and sent its devil to tempt us. Such minnows as we were not worthy of a visit from a significant shark. We were thus accorded a blond, blue-eyed, beefy bruiser in a stained silk shirt, a pale blue sports coat and a matching satin tie. His stickpin and cufflinks were enormous zircons, indicating he either thought large equaled good or that we would think so. Smiling broadly, revealing far less than Top Don dental work, our mobster marched directly to my husband's desk, slapped down a briefcase, and flipped it open to dazzle us with stacks of greenbacks. He then pulled a contract and a pen from his breast pocket and handed them to my husband with a flourish.

The minion of Mephistopheles was unprepared for my husband's response. Although very ill, JP was still very strong and highly experienced at dealing with thugs, having fought his way through and out of Brooklyn, N.Y. He grabbed the open briefcase and flung it out the door of the office, scattering bills throughout the parking lot. JP then grabbed the astonished crapo di tutti crappi, twisted one arm behind his back and shoved him across the parking lot, where he skidded face down on the asphalt several satisfying feet. Bloody, disheveled and terrified of being observed, the muscle head painfully dragged himself to his feet and staggered around the parking lot, futilely trying to gather up as much money as he could snatch from the breeze. Money flew everywhere, enriching astonished passers-by. Drawing a crowd, the grubby goon clambered into the back of his chauffeur driven black car and sped away.

The Castle Gargoyle

JP and I finished clearing out our office, shut the door on our dreams and drove with our boxes in our limping Lincoln to the Castle Argyle. The parking facility at the Castle was covered, but not gated or guarded. Almost no one who dwelled at the Argyle could afford to own a car, so there was plenty of room in the cavernous garage designed for the magnificent machines of the original occupants. Our car was likely the only one there that wasn't stolen.

JP and I spent the afternoon unloading the car and the rented truck that transported our large library and our otherwise slender possessions. In the early dusk we returned to the garage for one last box. There was the same mobster, swathed in bandages, scrapes colorfully painted with the bright red antiseptic of the time, sporting a new outfit, busily breaking into our trunk.

Working in daylight without gloves and without a guard at his back, this fellow was so pathetic we were certain his owners would soon have him put down. No doubt the lumpkin was expecting to find a box of incriminating business records to be used to coerce us into cooperating. He had just broken the trunk lock when my husband broke his arm and deposited him in the cactus patch outside the garage. Had he succeeded in opening the box in the trunk, he would have been greatly disappointed to find only a collection of 19th century French poetry.

We began our tenancy at the Castle without further disruption.

The Glory That Was Home

WHILE THE JUNKIES had stripped the Castle of nearly all salable objects by the time we arrived in the late 1960s, the derelict still trailed a few Wordsworthian clouds of glory. In my memory the lobby was a magnificent, soaring space, sunlit through a wall of French-paned windows. A few of the deep green velvet drapes that used to soften the walls still cascaded down in generous folds to rest on the huge squares of the burnished terra-cotta tile floor.

A stunning feature of the Castle was the tiny black wrought iron elevator with frosted beveled glass panels, resembling a Lalique jewel box. An ornate gilded shelf, over which hung a Baroque gilt-framed smoked crackle glass mirror, faced the elevator opening on every floor. Surely these once elegant shelves had held sumptuous bouquets of lush peonies and fragrant tuberoses and silver salvers for the calling cards of those courting the favor of stars and moguls.

Now the shelves were bare and defaced with messages scratched in with penknives, revealing a rich underlayment of red lacquer, so that the shelves appeared to be bleeding.

All the apartments I saw had ornately carved solid oak doors and leaded glass windows. Candle-drop wall sconces still lit the long halls. A wedding cake frosting of intricately hand-carved plaster cornices garlanded every inch of the passageways. The worn remains of the finest deep-pile cream wool carpeting with a faded pattern of ferns and flowers still cushioned footfalls throughout the building.

Our apartment was on a corner of the top floor, overlooking the freeway and the decaying stucco bungalows of old residential Hollywood. As we entered through our massive portal, stout enough to repel invading hordes, we stepped into an entry hall rising majestically to a fifteen foot ceiling and lined with inset Gothic-arched bookcases. Another Gothic archway opened onto the living room, richly carpeted wall-to-wall in pale sea-mist green wool frieze and large enough to swallow a Viennese ballroom. This was suited to the man who built the Castle, a wealthy Viennese physician, Alfred Guido Randolph Castles, colorful in early Hollywood history for his "glandular cure".

To the left off the foyer we walked into our huge kitchen to discover high glass-knobbed cupboards, white tile counters and a black and white checkerboard tile floor right out of a Felix Valloton painting. The kitchen led into the dining room where sufficient space awaited for a dinner party of twelve.

The dining and living rooms were lined with large windows, all of which opened outward. One living room window was an exquisite porthole, set like a jewel in the wall. The interlocking panes of opaque swirled glass spread outward like the petals of a flower when cranked with a little brass handle. Outside this wonderful window was an undeveloped lot heavily forested with towering old pines and spruce. This fragrant, cool space, silent but for bird song, provided us with a delightful respite from the oppressive heat, filthy air and roaring traffic that otherwise permeated the apartment.

Following the foyer to the right brought us to a huge bedroom and bathroom. Between the two was a charming built-in vanity table. The bedroom closet was large enough to be called a bedroom today.

Anonymously carved into one wall of the bedroom was the following admonition:

"Remember where you came from, where you are going and who you owe."

I have often wondered who penned, that is, knifed, this particularly valuable advice, having followed it all my life. It helped me keep my self and soul through those hard times, and many times after, and to remind me to be grateful to those who so generously helped us make our eventual escape from the Castle. The author surely must have been a humble person, someone who did not want to forget his or her original home, family and friends, should he or she either be stricken by sudden fame and fortune or crushed by failure, both of which were frequent in Hollywood. The author must also have had a firm grip on the harsh realities of the movie and music businesses, where powerful connections and financial backing are life and death. Whoever you are or were, I am grateful to you.

Fantasy Furnishings

WE CAME TO the Argyle with virtually nothing but our books. We had paid dearly to learn that healthcare could not care less and health insurance coverage did not cover. My husband's mysterious condition worsened, but he dragged himself to work, taking any sales job he could get from carbide tools to cemetery plots. I went to work as a secretary by day, a waitress by night and a ghost writer in between for advertising executives with fearsome deadlines. All the involved "health care providers" constantly encouraged us to stop working in order to render ourselves indigent so that we would qualify for assistance, meaning they could get paid faster than our faithful little monthly pittances could pay them.

We refused. My objective was to keep us afloat honorably and maintain for my husband at least minimal access to the quality of medical care that would never be available to a welfare patient. My husband's objective was to leave me a rich widow. This obstinate attitude rendered us too "wealthy" to qualify for any financial or physical assistance at all and too poor to do anything more than eat, pay rent, chip away at the granite mountain of our debts and feed the gaping maw of the medical Moloch.

Thus, we came to the Argyle with the only piece of furniture we had been unable to sell: a custom-made overstuffed white silk brocade sofa twelve feet long, a white elephant if ever there was one. However, the sumptuous space of our living room dwarfed the mighty divan; it cowered against the wall like a doll house miniature.

All the rare books and the finer first editions from our personal and professional libraries had already gone. This left us with approximately 1,500 lesser volumes that quickly overwhelmed the beautiful bookcases of the foyer. We stacked many of the leftover tomes to form a dining table, coffee table, benches and end tables. Other works of literature formed night stands on either side of our "bed," the space on the rug between the stacks. We used the lining of my husband's old trench coat as a table cloth for the "dining table" and the coat for a blanket on our "bed." Several years later, we ceremonially buried this sacred protector at sea, by moonlight, off the coast of Santa Barbara.

The remaining books loomed in a massive pile rivaling the Pyramid of Cheops. Buying shelving was out of the question in our budget, so we went scavenging. Neighborhood renovation provided scrap lumber and discarded cans of black lacquer allowed us to dress the boards. We hauled lovely old time-softened bricks from an abandoned foundation to make student-style shelving. This produced very attractive housing for the books all around the walls of the living room and the foyer.

Our kitchen equipment at move-in was nearly as limited as our supply of furniture. We possessed a two-cup stovetop Vesuvio espresso pot dating from my husband's European operatic adventures 25 years before, two espresso cups, a single Copenhagen dinner plate, a frail mouth-blown glass carafe and a chipped Majolica divided serving platter. Fortunately, my husband's impecunious youth had refined him in the crucible of necessity, rendering him an expert thrift store shopper. The Assistance League Thrift Shop on Vermont Street in Los Angeles provided us with serviceable essentials and two gems, a 1910 pyramidal toaster and a 1930 egg poacher with Queen Anne legs.

After about two weeks of sleeping on our hardwood "bed" and dining on our "table," our welfare-defying paychecks enabled us to hunt for used furniture. We needed a bed, a dining table and two chairs, at the absolute minimum. Our budget to furnish the entire apartment and pay for delivery was $500, at the absolute maximum. JP sleuthed out the warehouse in Los Angeles where the Bekins Van and Storage Company stored for sale furniture of poor souls who had been unable to pay their storage or cross-country moving bills. The warehouse was a musty catacomb, a multi-storied tomb of-doom-and-gloom where the sad shards of unfortunate lives had been cast as if into an ossuary. Digging in this pauper's grave, parting the shrouds of cobwebs and coughing from the disturbed dust, we found long-buried treasure.

Tightly stacked and imprisoned with a grimy rope was a matched suite of hardwood furniture thickly covered with dirt. Hand-sweeping revealed a large bed, a drop-leaf table with six high-backed leather-seated chairs, a carved sideboard and a charming little drop-front writing desk. After tense negotiations with their captors, their ransom, including delivery, came to exactly $500. We were overjoyed as our furniture ascended to our apartment from the Castle garage in the ponderously slow service elevator that once carried cases of champagne and caviar. Murphy's Wood Soap, rich wax polish and hours of elbow grease restored dignity to our furniture and comfort to us. We dined seated on our chairs at our table and then collapsed blissfully into our soft bed.

The Secret of the Dusty Desk

WE PLACED THE little desk in the foyer under the only available light, a frosted Deco wall fixture. While cleaning the interior of the desk, we found faded photographs of a wealthy couple appearing to be about 70 years of age in various stages of a pre-World War I European tour. Steeped as I was in British mysteries wherein the clues to the family fortune are found on crumpled notes hidden in the dark recesses of the victim's desk, I could not resist poking my fingers all the way to the back of each pigeon hole in turn. I said dramatically to JP: "Now I am going to pull out a bank book full of money."

I pulled out a bank book full of money. The little dark blue book stated it had been the property of a woman, whose last recorded deposit had been made in 1923. Folded inside the book were two pristine five dollar bills, dated series of 1928 and 1934, respectively. We both immediately felt that the bank book, the $10 and all the furniture rightfully belonged to her heirs. Resignedly, we kissed our furniture good-bye and set out to find her tribe.

The bank book gave the Beverly Hills address of a Corinthian-columned pile. We called upon an astonished V.P. at what proved to be the sixth successor bank. He was sufficiently intrigued to dig into a vault of moldering ledgers, wherein he found a connection to relations who still had accounts with his bank. We gave him our telephone number, left the bank book and the money with him, and asked him to offer the furniture to the family for the $500 we had paid for it. The grim vision of again slurping our gruel atop our two-volume 1880 edition of Rawlinson's 1846 History of Ancient Egypt and sleeping on the hard floor spoiled our appetite and rest that night.

An agonizing two weeks passed before we received a very curt call from an irritated elderly male voice, advising us that the family had not the faintest interest in some silly bank book with its paltry $10 and wanted nothing whatsoever to do with some scruffy old furnishings. We could chuck everything in the garbage for all he cared and do not bother us further, haaarrrumph, slam! Elated, we called upon the banker to thank him. We gave him the bank book for the records and he gave us the $10, which we put back in the pigeon hole when we happily returned home to what was now truly our furniture.

The table evolved over time into a work desk and eventually a computer station, finally collapsing in exhaustion in 2002. The chairs, the decaying leather seats of which proved to be stuffed with horsehair and newspapers advertising bustles, buggies and Lydia Pinkham's potion, were given in the 1980s to someone who could afford to restore them. We gave the bed to someone who had the large space it required when we moved on to life in apartments smaller than the bed. The sideboard and the little desk with its secret cache are with us today, as beautiful and sturdy as ever.

The Night of the Gilded Guests

WHAT DO YOU do when you are broke, in debt, sick and hopeless? You give a party, of course. We had the good fortune to know interesting people from all walks of life in Southern California. Some of them were even good enough friends to invite to a party where the libations would be espresso and jug wine, the viands dubious cheese, failing fruit and day-old baguettes and the only entertainment the antics of our newly-acquired kitten.

Born in an apartment down the hall, her screaming at our door brought us running. She promptly pulled herself up JP's clothes to his shoulder and nestled against his head. She was black velvet plush with the huge ears of Egyptian forbears. JP named her Ptah, recognizing in her the qualities of the chief god of Memphis, embodying great strength and life force, worshiped as The Shaper of the World. Also, the name was reflective of her mighty roar, designed to frighten her slaves into submission. This was not a hiss or a yowl, but rather an explosive blast: "Phhhhhhhhaaaaaaaaa!"

I no longer remember the name of all the guests at the party, but four are still clear and dear in my mind. There were the wonderful actor and fine photographer, Horst Ebersberg, and his talented actress/singer/dancer wife, Judy Rollin. Horst was, happily for his bank account, but unhappily for his aspirations, invariably typecast as various Nazi officers. Judy was at the time on the chocolate cake diet, then popular in Hollywood, and brought her supply with her. This was promptly confiscated for dessert.

Another guest who prefers anonymity was a fascinating adventurer, who lived by his wits and his remarkable linguistic abilities. His past was known only to himself; we believed he had escaped from Russia and worked his way all over the world. His knowledge of the people, art, customs and history of many countries could have filled volumes.

Best-beloved of invitees was Hanna Frenkel, who has remained our cherished friend all these nearly 40 years and whose 90th birthday we celebrated on November 7, 2004. Hanna can truly say she "knew us when," having welcomed me into her family when I arrived in California at the age of 20 to conquer the world. Wherever her relations have established themselves in the world, from New York to California, in Israel, Australia, England, Europe and Asia, they have contributed as distinguished scholars and professors, prominent religious leaders, international emissaries, brilliant businesspeople and generous humanitarians. JP and I are honored that Hanna counts us among her closest friends.

In preparation for our party, I undertook to make our decaying bathroom fixtures look as clean as they actually were. I was horrified to find that no amount of scrubbing and sterilizing would improve the appearance of our very old, rusty, chipped, deeply stained toilet. I decided to disguise the disgusting hulk by spraying gold paint on the seat and gluing huge fake rubies, sapphires and emeralds all over the tank. Thus, we could call it the proverbial "Throne" and raise scatological humor to new heights. I set to work with paint and jewels early in the morning the day of the party.

The paint was guaranteed to dry in twelve hours. My husband and I used my completed work of art very carefully, touching none of the surfaces, during this drying time. When I welcomed our guests that evening, I relished the secret satisfaction that we would not be embarrassed by what would have appeared to have been a filthy fixture.

The evening was wonderful, made so by the group of bright, interesting people, who exchanged with extreme civility their disparate views of philosophy, art, history, politics and myriad other topics. Our favorite Baroque chamber music and candles provided the atmosphere, and the food, wine and coffee were spread out on a huge garage sale coffee table. Ptah, endlessly petted and passed from lap to lap by adoring sycophants, charmingly destroyed nylon stockings, knit skirts, silk blouses and leather handbags.

Throughout the evening, as coffee and wine consumption dictated, the guests one by one visited the bathroom. Delighted laughter rang out as the Throne was discovered, reported and photographed.

Exhausted and happy, the yawning guests eventually

drifted out the door. We left Ptah blissfully curled against the warm espresso pot and collapsed into bed.

Late the next morning, we received several phone calls from guests, who informed us that their spouses and significant others had discovered golden cheeks…

St. Francis of Argyle

Over time at the Castle, JP's condition slowly, but inexorably, grew worse. The tumor gnawed at his creative brilliance, his judgment, business acumen, physical functions, short-term memory and personality. He suffered increasingly from nausea, vertigo, fatigue, blurred vision, broken concentration, severe migraines, blackouts and painful muscle spasms. He was to endure these horrors until October 1975 when a physician possessed of courage and splendid ethics defied the cruel rules and admitted JP to a hospital normally reserved for the fortunate few covered by health insurance. With less than an hour of life left him, the newly-invented brain scanning device allowed JP's tumor to be seen for the first time and successfully removed.

We have been grateful every day of our lives since to the wonderful admitting physician, who would accept no money, and the generous neurosurgical team whose members cut their bills in half. Owing to the barbaric health insurance system in this country, it took us more than 20 years to pay off these and related massive medical expenses.

Through all the years the tumor was pressing on his brain, JP somehow remained extremely gentle. He was never aggressive or physically violent, but did have tumor and PTSD-inspired volcanic verbal outbursts that sometimes frightened people. Not so four-legged animals, however. Particularly during the time we lived at the Castle Argyle, they were drawn to him in a most remarkable way.

Just as Ptah had selected our door from among many others, pulled herself up to JP's shoulder and clung to his head, animals of all sorts were attracted to him. Every cat, domestic and feral, in and around the Argyle would follow him, weave in and out his legs and cling to his neck and shoulders. Lost, sick and injured dogs of every size and type would flock to him when he sat outside, the smaller curling up in his arms, the larger leaning against his legs with their heads on his knees.

Wild birds, including starlings, sparrows and robins, would land on his head, dig their feet into his hair and stay there until other people approached. Escaped cage birds, with injured wings or missing a leg, would land on his shoes and nestle down between his feet with no fear of being crushed. In this way we acquired our two gimpy canaries, Pernod, as deep a yellow as the liqueur, and Pompadour, whose topknot resulted from being pecked by healthy birds. They lived happily with us for the rest of their lives, trilling to Bach and adding coloratura to JP's tenor.

It was amazing enough to see animals flocking to JP,

but what was truly astounding is that on many occasions *all of these creatures sat together with him in complete silence and perfect harmony.* They must have sensed he was as sick, pained, frightened and confused as they. They must have known that in spite of his loud, angry expressions he was absolutely harmless, completely without aggression toward them, unlike a normal human being—one of them. He was also somehow an ark, an island where the iron law of nature that decreed prey and predator, friend and foe, fearsome and feared was somehow suspended. The lion lay down with the lamb and Edward Hicks' 1833 painting of The Peaceable Kingdom came to life before my eyes.

If only all people could somehow achieve the same state, in which would be absent the usual greed, lust for power and willingness to harm others to achieve personal ends. We might then, at last, achieve world peace.

These experiences with animals continued until JP's tumor was removed. He has always loved animals and most animals like him, but nothing like the former affinity has occurred since our time at the Castle. Passing dogs sniff his hand, wag their tales mildly and travel on. Feral cats run from him as they do from everyone and no birds approach. One of our household cats loves to sleep on his bed, but no more than she does mine, while the other does not like to be petted or picked up by him at all. He is one of us now and no longer one of them.

JP's injury site is expected to develop another tumor, but so slowly it will not bother him before he reaches about 110, according to our neurosurgeon. However, should the tumor try to fool us, the animals will tell us.

The Art Mart on the Pyre of Fire

MANY OF THE lost souls who existed in the dreary dens of the Argyle's basement made their living by stealing and selling art and antiques. JP and I discovered their steerage deck when we descended to the storage room at the invitation of the manager to help ourselves to any of the possessions abandoned by tenants who had died, disappeared over night or been evicted. The bottom dwellers scuttled off at our approach, wary of anyone who looked establishment enough to have connections to authority.

Most of them were teenagers from the mid-west who had climbed off the Greyhound clutching battered guitar cases, hoping to become rock stars. Within a week of arrival they would be broke and playing on Hollywood Boulevard for enough money to eat and share a room with several others like them. When life became unbearable, they took up theft to buy enough drugs to make life just bearable enough not to go home failures.

Deep in the bowels of the building, JP and I groped our way through the unlit storage room, a dank hole filled with eerie silence and pitiful ends, and hauled out two barely usable dressers. Most everything else was beyond repair, but for a beautiful mahogany tobacco stand and some very high-quality briar pipes, all in perfect condition. (It took over 40 years to solve the mystery of these pipes, but you will find out in the Epilogue.) We were momentarily astonished the junkies had not discovered them, then realized that, of course, these items had been stolen and stashed with many others, awaiting sale for drug money.

We had learned that the Argyle addicts were sponsored in their enterprise by a few bent officers of the law. The junkies stole the goods while the perverted policemen looked the other way, in exchange for 50% of the take and protecting the thieves from arrest.

In addition to hiding stolen objects in the basement room, the junkies stashed the paintings, sculpture and antique furniture in what were called "garbage closets," stinking, fetid rooms at the end of every hallway where tenants deposited their trash for pickup, theoretically weekly. These repulsive rooms were located close to the openings of the elevator and the staircase, providing easy access. The stolen goods were protected by large plastic sheets and camouflaged with masses of rotting garbage no one was likely to disturb. The garbage truck driver must have had a piece of the action, as some of the larger antiques moved in and out via the garbage truck.

The Castle Gargoyle

Art & Antique Enterprises, Inc. went along smoothly until an internal investigation in the police department exposed the bad cops. Acting on a tip, the investigators timed a night raid to catch them in the act. Suddenly the Castle was besieged by police cars, all screaming sirens, flashing lights and screeching brakes. Uniforms with drawn guns raved through bullhorns, causing the neighbors to gather outside and everyone in the Castle to run to the windows and pour into the hallways. As the good cops raced up the staircase, the bad cops and the junkies worked furiously to pull incriminating items out of the garbage closets and fling them out of the back windows onto a huge bonfire, hastily set with gasoline on an asphalt strip near the forested lot.

Feasting on oil paints and dry Chippendale, the flames leapt up, starting a crown fire in the nearest resin-filled pine tree. By now residents and neighbors in their nightclothes were screaming and massing in the street. Jumping junkies and distraught dealers scattered in every direction, as did terrified prostitutes and their half-clad customers, who thought the police were cracking down on them. The good cops milled around hopelessly, yelling at the seething mass of people, having no idea whom to arrest as everyone frantically tried to pull precious things from the pyre. Some of this was possibly altruistic, but we were certain that some of the liberated items found their way to new homes that evening.

In the meantime fire trucks roared up, turning the hoses at full blast on the pine torch, the bonfire, the police and the raving mob, then coating everything and everyone with foam fire retardant, resulting in a mound resembling a gigantic parfait. By the time the fire was out, the good cops had arrested and hauled off some of the actual miscreants and inadvertently a few of the outraged neighbors. The fire trucks drove off, the neighbors drifted home under cover of darkness with suspicious bulges beneath their bathrobes, the junkies, dealers, prostitutes, pimps and customers returned to their accustomed haunts and thus ended evening. What a shame that this was not filmed for a movie.

JP and I read the blazing headlines the next day, declaring that the long-standing corruption in the police department had at last been rooted out. A large photograph a few days later in the follow-up story showed self-satisfied official types shaking hands and awarding commendations. On the wall behind the desk of a dignitary I recognized a beautiful oil painting. It was gratifying to see it had not been damaged by the fire.

Escape from the Dungeon

WITH GENEROUS FINANCIAL help from my parents and very hard work, JP and I made our way out of the Castle. Most who lived there then were not as fortunate, dying of overdoses and broken hearts or just disappearing in the night without a trace. I hope at least some found their way home.

The Castle Argyle, beautifully restored, is now a highly respectable residence for seniors, a perfect function for such a Grand Dame of old Hollywood. I shall remind her of her past no further.

Epilogue 2013

Almost Gone With The Gargoyle: The Mystery of Clark *Gable*'s Magnificent Sasieni Briars

Forty-six years have passed since my husband and I came to the Castle and descended into the junk-room in search of anything usable. This dark, dank hole mainly held the moldy detritus of four decades of disadvantaged tenants' sorry possessions, consisting mainly of three-legged tables, seatless chairs and broken lamps. We searched in vain for a dresser with at least one drawer.

Steering clear of the tarp covering the stash of newly-stolen goods the tenant junkies kept for sale, I gingerly made my way through the gloom with only a dim flashlight. I tripped over a small floor-model tobacco stand, all its details obscured beneath a thick shroud of viscous dust, clearly undisturbed since 349 B.C. Close by on the floor were a desktop humidor and a rack of three pipes, equally encrusted. My husband and I both smoked and collected pipes, so under normal circumstances, we would have recognized a treasure when we saw it. Expecting nothing of quality whatsoever, I still could not resist carrying the filthy things upstairs to check them out.

Lord Carnarvon's astonishment upon discovering King Tut's tomb was nothing compared to ours when we realized what we had unearthed. The table-top humidor proved to be beautifully made of mahogany with interior sides of cedar and a zinc-lined lid. Fans of old movies will recognize an identical humidor on Sam Spade's desk in the 1941 noir classic, The Maltese Falcon, based on the novel by Dashiell Hammett, directed by John Huston and starring Humphrey Bogart, Sidney Greenstreet and Peter Lorrie. I entertained the fanciful notion that this might be that very humidor, purloined from the film set by a pipe-smoking property manager and secreted in his then elegant suite at the Castle. (Research later proved the actual humidor was the property of Jack's, one of the finest and oldest restaurants in San Francisco, where Dashiell Hammett was known to dine, sadly stolen from the display case a few years before this writing.)

But the rest of the treasure trove was real: three briar pipes that are among the earliest hand-carved by Joel Sasieni in London, England, who began carving in 1919. The oldest of the three is a signed Sasieni One-Dot bearing Great Britain Patent No. 150221, granted on September 2, 1920. The next verifiable Sasieni is an Eight-Dot bearing his U.S.

Patent No. 1,513,428, granted October 28, 1924. The third pipe, unfortunately showing no patent number, is also an Eight-Dot, bearing the words "London Made" and signed by Sasieni. My fellow members of the North American Society of Pipe Collectors and knowledgeable pipe folks throughout the world acknowledge Sasienis as among the very finest pipes ever created.

Now to the mystery of who might have owned these remarkable pipes and how they came to their ignominious grave in the tomb of the Castle's basement. It was obvious upon examination that the pipes had been smoked with extreme care, with expert knowledge of loading and lighting, over a long period of time. I knew that Clark Gable had been prominent among the luminaries who had lived at the Castle in the heyday of Hollywood movie-making. I also knew that his Sasienis were among his most beloved personal possessions. But, given this, how would they have come to their basement burial? To a pipe collector, this was akin to the dumping of Mozart's body in an unmarked lime-pit in the paupers' graveyard.

Three possibilities occurred to me at the time. Firstly, the Sasienis could have been stolen and stashed while Clark Gable was temporarily elsewhere, but it was not likely his suite would have been unattended in his absence. Secondly, packers could simply have overlooked the pipes when Clark Gable moved away from Hollywood, but that is highly unlikely, even though he had others, given that Sasienis were known to be among his favorite things. The third possibililty is that something monumentally disruptive occurred in his life, something that outweighed everything else. I suggest this was the sudden death of his beloved wife, Carol Lombard, on January 16, 1942.

But how to prove any of this? I do not believe there is any way to prove how these splendid works of art came to be flung into the Castle graveyard. But I was at last able to prove that one of the pipes was indeed Clark Gable's. My friend, pipe and cigar specialist Marty Pulvers, came upon the spring 1999 edition of Pipes and Tobaccos Magazine. The cover is a magnificent studio photograph of Clark Gable smoking one of his favorite Sasienis, one of the two Eight-Dots, recognizable in the absolute when compared for shape, grain and pattern with the actual pipe. "There is your pipe," said Marty. No two briar grain patterns are exactly alike. I think we can safely believe the other two pipes were Clark Gable's as well.

These splendid pieces of old Hollywood now live in state in the collection of a friend with a penchant for cinema memorabilia and tobacciana. I bet you can't talk him out of them at any price, but you can see the Gable cover photo by Googling Clark Gable, Sasieni, Pipes and Tobaccos Magazine.

*Part of this story was originally printed in the February 2009 edition of The Pipe Collector, the journal of The North American Society of Pipe Collectors. The editors have kindly granted permission to reprint it here.

ODD JOBS

TIPS FOR TOUGH TIMES

Help Wanted!

People who are motivated to do or learn whatever is needed to keep the dollars coming in to support themselves.

Interested??

Inquire Within.

DANA GRAE KANE

For Christine.

Motivations

OLD GEEZERS SUCH as I (68) and especially older geezers will shudder at the memory of the Crash of 1929 and the Great Depression of the 1930s. "It was so terrible and lasted so long we could never forget it," said my mother. Her pioneer family lost everything scratched out of the ground since the first of the clan got off the boat in 1619, a year before the *Mayflower* docked. The eldest of four children, my mother became at age 14 an income-producing adult, contributing vitally to the household by cooking, scrubbing, and babysitting for more fortunate people. This she did throughout high school, while maintaining highest honors. It was painfully clear to her that there would be no money for college, so she buried her dreams and took typing, shorthand, and bookkeeping. Following graduation, she worked as a secretary/court reporter/full-charge bookkeeper by day and a seamstress/cook/waitress by night.

Throughout the Depression, my mother never turned down an offer of legitimate paid work. When the WPA[1] began paying 50 cents per night to teach French, she signed up immediately, even though she knew not one syllable of French or any related language. Teaching herself from the course book, she stayed one lesson ahead of the class. In her 94 years of life, I never heard her utter a single word of self-pity or complaint about how hard she had to work in those harrowing times. What she said was: "Our family was very lucky; we had good skills to sell."

Too many of you are experiencing your own personal Great Depression, having lost your job, your health insurance, your home, or all three. My personal Great Depression clobbered me at age 22 when my husband's "pre-existing" medical conditions, stemming from injuries and a hidden brain tumor, rendered him uninsurable for most of the next 40 years. You stop paying the bills, the treatment stops. Health-noncare that could not care less. I, like countless others, had three bad choices: (1) sink financially until my husband qualified for free but inferior welfare medical care, (2) turn him over to the VA where the treatment for the then mysterious PTSD was electroshock followed by lobotomy, of which he was justifiably terrified, or (3) find ways to earn enough money to provide the best possible care. His only chance was (3).

I always had to make more money than I was educated

---

[1] The Works Progress Administration, created by President Franklin D. Roosevelt in 1937 to provide paid work for unemployed artists and writers, later expanded to put people to work on vital infrastructure projects.

to earn. All those years, I had to work two jobs or a full-time job with consistent overtime. I had to get and hold jobs for which I often had no training, no experience, and little or no natural aptitude. My mother's example guided me. Some wonderful people I met along the way, some of whom you will meet in this book, helped me immeasurably.

Invaluable assistance in creating this book came from editors Jill Kelly and Fern Sophia, who made suggestions on the final version, manuscript-polisher Lorrie Schnabler and electronic document formatter Charlotte Creel. They will convince you I am a much better writer than I actually am. Any errors you find are there because I stubbornly ignored their advice.

Don't give up; get up and get creative. I assure you there is always a way. Some of the jobs I did felt like prison sentences for crimes I didn't commit, but they paid the bills and kept my husband alive. There is always a way. You may not like the way, but there is always a way. I found several ways. I hope this book helps you find them, too

Counter Attack

Help someone else and someone may help you.

At age 20, I hopped in my $150 '52 Chevy and blazed south. I left Portland, Oregon for Los Angeles, there to seek my fortune as a writer and join my boyfriend, already there seeking his. I had just enough money to last a month, so immediately upon arrival I began flinging my résumé around the Wilshire Boulevard financial center, where the best-paying secretarial jobs lived. I was a very realistic writer who liked to eat every day.

One day, job-hunting Boyfriend was dining from the bottom of the menu at a Wilshire high-rise lunch counter. His concentration was entirely devoted to praying he could dig up $1.25 to pay his bill. While clawing at his pocket lint, he accidentally elbowed a frail-looking, older man on the next stool, who toppled onto the marble floor. Boyfriend dropped to his knees, cradled the man's head in his lap, apologized profusely, and shouted for someone to call an ambulance. A horrific sequence of fatal injury through financial disaster to involuntary manslaughter conviction raced through Boyfriend's mind. Just then the resilient man chuckled and sat up, apparently unscathed, saying "Not to worry, young fellow. I've fallen off these stools before; my medical condition affects my balance."

Boyfriend helped the old gent to his feet and offered to walk him wherever he needed to go, embarrassed to be unable to afford a cab. The very humble, beautifully spoken, plainly dressed man, replied that his office was just upstairs in the same building. Boyfriend concluded by the man's neat, unassuming attire that the poor soul probably sorted mail, at best. However, at least the guy had a job.

They entered the elevator, which to Boyfriend's astonishment went not down to a subterranean mail processing warren but up to the penthouse suite. The brass letters above the massive doors announced the West Coast headquarters of a major U.S. empire. As they entered the office, the receptionist exclaimed: "Oh, we were so worried. You really mustn't go out by yourself in your condition." Concerned executives came running from every part of the office. The "mail clerk" was the boss.

Mr. Big introduced dazed Boyfriend to his staff and then guided him to a deep leather chair in front of a huge desk in a corner office with a view of the known world. "Now, young man," said Mr. Big, "What may I do for you?"

Boyfriend, astonished and overwhelmed, blurted out the most impressive thing he could think of: "My girlfriend interpreted for the President of France. She needs a job!"

While this nanosecond of glory classed-up my résumé, that and 35 cents would buy me a cup of coffee. (This was the pre-Starbuckian, just after the Jurassic.)

"What else can she do?" asked Mr. Big. Boyfriend then recovered himself enough to stammer out my secretarial experience, explaining I had typed my way through high school and college. Mr. Big immediately picked up the phone and called the major brokerage firm downstairs.

Instantly put through to the Managing Director, Mr. Big greeted him jovially by first name and announced: "I just found your new secretary." I started the next morning.

While I did not get this job on my own merits, I had to be competent enough to keep it and not embarrass the person who recommended me. Bear in mind, when a contact goes out on a limb for you, and you saw the limb off, that contact will and should never touch so much as a twig for you again.

Now I was secretary to six stockbrokers, making more money than I had ever seen. It was the no-holds-barred heyday of insider information, manipulated IPOs and offshore tax havens where billions were made, lost, and remade several times daily. We worked on New York time, so I had to be there, ready to roar, by 6.

After I had been with the firm about a month, the manager announced a $100 prize for the first person who could come up with an idea that would save the firm time and money, yet cost the firm nothing to implement. $100 in that day covered rent for a month, plus groceries for a week, and a lobster dinner out. Thus motivated, I submitted my proofreading system, which I had devised many jobs ago for proofing numbers. I invented this system as a method of keeping myself from making mistakes due to boredom-induced brain death.

This simple technique cuts in half the time necessary to proof tedious columns of figures on List B against master List A. Brokerage businesses deal with masses of numbers identifying transactions, stock certificates, and prices. Staying out of prison depends on accurate numerical records. Accurate records require accurate proofing. I could taste lobster.

I hereby bequeath you the secrets of my system. Working with two parallel columns of figures, my simple method eliminates the constant motion required to shift the proofer's eyes from left to right, then back to the left again before beginning to read the next set of numbers. Making a motion back to the left takes at least one second per shift and breaks concentration. Instead, a proofer can read the first set of numbers from left to right in the usual way, then, without shifting his or her eyes back to the left, drop straight down to the next set and read from right to left, then drop down to the next set and read from left to right again, and so on. A number is the same number whether you read the digits left to right or right to left. I always worked with a ruler or an envelope under the line of numbers I was reading. After taking the Evelyn Wood Reading Dynamics course, I could proof without moving my eyes from side to side at all. I was able to see both columns simultaneously in one visual field.

Not only did I pocket the $100 dollars, I received a raise. That was great, but the most valuable thing I gained from this job was the financial vocabulary that enabled me later on to land a job producing a newsletter for another prominent brokerage firm. My only regret is having invested in the lobster dinner instead of shares in up-and-coming companies. *Sic transit crustacea.*

This experience taught me how important it is to study different businesses, figure out what it is they do and what would likely be useful to them, and suggest it when applying for a job in that field. Even if the particular business already does what you suggest or does not need it at all, the fact that you bothered to research and present the idea may, in the eyes of a jaded interviewer, set you apart from the other 1,000 candidates who are just looking to suck a salary plus benefits from the company. You are too, of course, but you won't be as obvious as some other applicants.

You can profit from my worst mistake ever in a job interview. The interviewer at what I realized too late was a world-renowned enterprise asked very proudly: "Do you know what we do?" I, idiot, replied, "No; tell me about it." He told me where to find the door.

Get up, coffee up, show up first and innovate, even at the crummy job you are dying to dump. Someone you know there may be leaving for a better job and take you along. At the very least, you will get a rave reference for your next application.

The Bank Job

Offer value beyond the job description.

Having survived working for the *nouveau riche* of L.A., I evaded the border patrol and slipped into Beverly Hills. This was the land of Old Family Money, New Money desperate to look like Old Family Money, old families desperate to hide that they had run out of money, and climbers who had never had any money trying to weasel money from the other three. Remnants thrice-removed from European and Russian royalty offered defunct titles in exchange for the hands of commoners with trust funds.

The VP of Public Relations at a small, exclusive bank needed a secretary to help him communicate with all the above types of connivers, attract those with actual money to the bank, and speak French with those who felt it elevated them to do so. Ah, snobbery! I could always count on it. An experimental scholarship in early childhood had provided me with the opportunity to study French and in high school I gained two years of Spanish. I maintained my language skills throughout college and after, although I never really believed they would actually be useful. It just seemed a shame to lose any hard-earned skill on the off-chance an unexpected opportunity might arise.

While my daily duties encompassed all the usual clerical drudgery, I was often asked to represent the bank at Chamber of Commerce business development functions where there would be, for example, the French Consul General, representatives of French product lines and French travel industry executives, all wooing Old and New Money.

One such function involved a luncheon at a restaurant at the adjacent marina. The restaurateur was introducing his new French chef and gourmet menu to Chamber members by providing a four-hour, eight-course meal with an appropriate wine to accompany every course. The restaurateur, a client of the bank, asked my boss if I would come and translate the names of the exotic dishes on the menu for the pinstripes in attendance. Given that the local business lunch crowd was accustomed to gulping greasy burgers with onion rings and racing back to the office, you can see where Escargots de Something with St. What's-its 1957 vintage served over a leisurely four hours would be a new and exciting experience for them.

This sounded like a pleasant, easy task and I anticipated a nice lunch to boot. The only difficulty would be the eight wine courses. A mere thimble-full of alcohol renders me groggy immediately. I did not wish to put myself in any jeopardy and certainly did not wish to embarrass the bank.

My plan was simply to turn my eight goblets over as the steward made the rounds. However, when I arrived, reality struck.

I would be standing behind a podium on a raised dais, expected to explain to the diners what they were eating, pronounce the name on the label of each bottle in turn, and then take a sip of and expound richly upon the virtues of each wine as it was poured out. No lunch for me and no way to avoid the venomous vintage. So much for the best-laid plans of mice and tea-totaling interpreters. I should have remembered there is no such thing as a free lunch. Never, not ever.

The luncheon began with the chef and the owner flanking me at the head of the room. I greeted the chef in fulsome French, he responded in delighted-be-here English and bowed to the diners, who applauded and polished off their pre-lunch libations, carried from the bar. The owner then went off to a table at the back of the room, the chef repaired to the kitchen, and the first course was served and poured. I described the artistry of the delicately crafted casaba boats with prosciutto sails and took the tiniest sip possible of the accompanying Wine #1. The grapes immediately began to turn to vinegar in my empty stomach, while I pronounced their names and invented something about their matchless bouquet. There followed leek and potato soup with Wine #2, filet of some unfortunate fish with #3, palate-cleansing sorbet with #4, chicken-casserole with #5, and palate-cleansing redux via salad with #6. By the time we reached this arrangement of what might have been two tiny *haricots verts* on a lettuce leaf, I was leaning against the podium to stay upright and the guests were roaring drunk, having swilled most of each course of wine cushioned by only the miniscule *nouvelle cuisine* portions of food.

My head reeled and the room swayed as I mumbled something about the cheese and crackers with #7. By the time we reached the chocolate mousse with dessert wine #8, I have no idea what nonsense I might have blathered. Fortunately, everyone there was so plastered they understood nothing anyway and no longer noticed me at all. As the raucous, swaying mob stumbled out the door, some singing naughty GI-French ditties from WWII, I clutched the railing around the marina and staggered into a cab, going directly home to bed.

Fortunately, the next day at the bank brought nothing but compliments from the restaurateur who, having been swacked himself, recalled nothing, freeing him to believe the event was a great success. The glories of French cuisine and wine had similarly descended upon the members of the Chamber of Commerce who, once their terrible headaches dissipated, congratulated each other on having greatly upgraded the tourist area with the addition of a sophisticated French dining facility. The restaurateur maintained his account at the Bank and conferred with me about Edith Piaf recordings for his dining room, and I kept my job another day.

> *Always keep your skills up no matter how useless*
> *they may seem. You will have them at the ready*
> *when your chance comes. Someone else won't.*

The Pizza House Bar Grill and Family Restaurant

Apply for a job no one else wants so that lack of experience doesn't matter.

THE BILLS WERE big in '68. The secretarial pittance paid by the swank bank didn't make a dent in the medical invoice mountain. Boyfriend and I had parted amicably in 1966 and I had met, gone into business with and married The Man for Me in 1967. We had sworn the sickness/health-richer/poorer oath. We got the sickness and poorer. He bore the aftermath of multiple serious injuries, including a blow to the head at age 9, a BB gun shot that blinded one eye at age 15 and the rest from military service in two wars as a young adult. He suffered severe migraines, intermittent black-outs and variably blurred vision in the remaining good eye. I was prepared to help him deal with all of this.

Naively, I planned to cover him as my dependent on my health insurance. But I was clueless as to the implications of the two little weasel words "pre-existing condition." Only a few private policies costing about $4,000 per month with yearly increases would even consider taking him to their cash-lined bosoms. I made what was then an extremely good clerical salary: $500 per month. In the meantime, my brilliant business partner/loving husband went stark raving mad. Invisible to X-rays, a benign brain tumor was lurking. Eight long years went by before the then newly-invented brain scanner revealed it.

I answered an ad for a night-shift waitress at a dump on Hollywood Boulevard, on the wrong side of the tracks in L.A. I needed to find a hole where no one from the bank would be caught dead. If recognized, I would be fired from the bank, pronto. Also, I had to locate a joint so desperate for a waitress that they'd hire someone faking experience.

"Pizza House Bar Grill and Family Restaurant" proclaimed the scabrous sign in the fervent hope that not a single potential patron among the bottom-dwellers of nighttime Hollywood would be lost. The grease-encrusted neon beer blinker in the window provided the only light on the street.

I pushed through the door into the bar. There hunkered the regulars over beer and meatball sandwiches, blearly eyeballs glued to the overhead TV. The bartender proved to be the swilling son of Mr. and Mrs. Owner. Owner Jr. slurped up more of the profits than the barflies could replenish. Owner Sr. was a senile 80-something, drooling at a dim corner table. Mrs. Owner, who was a marvelous cook and deserved far better, single-handedly slaved in the kitchen and ran the business. She took one look at me in my banker-friendly three-piece gray garb, sighed in sad resignation, and hired me immediately at minimum wage plus tips. As I had hoped, no one else had applied. From now on, I would have to race home from the bank, whip off my daytime disguise, fling myself into a black skirt, white shirt and apron from the thrift shop, and somehow make it to work on time. Thus began my clandestine night-life.

There was one wonderful thing about this place and that was The Waiter, a magnificent human being and a superb Ritz-level hotel server. This marvelous man generously covered all my ineptitude and taught me enough to survive the job. He could carry five heavy platters of slippery, steaming pasta on one arm while pouring the house rotgut, all the while extolling the mythical merits of the swill, without spilling a drop of anything. It was clear to me that discrimination had forced him to sink to this place. Even in Hollywood, openly gay men were still untouchables in the '60s.

Customers were few and far between, so The Waiter and I used to pass the down-time playing chess in the supply alcove at the back of the dining area. Here hulked a massive refrigerator, on top of which we piled pulpy old phone books and tomato crates. We perched on these out of sight but still able to judge just when to climb down, refill coffee, present the check and pray someone would leave a $1 bill on the table for us to split.

Thanks to that partnership, I managed to withstand six months at that dive, reaching my personal best of $5.25 in tips my last night before leaving for a better night job.

Be open to every possibility. Never pass up an opportunity just because it is not exactly what you want. Make the most of it by learning all you possibly can and move on.

Life or Death

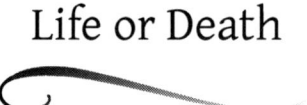

Look for ways to relieve someone else's desperation.

MY HUSBAND WAS by now in nearly constant pain from blinding migraines, dizzy, nauseous, delusional, erratic, uncertain as to whom I might be and requiring caretakers. I needed to find something better-paying than the bank job. This is where I learned to look for jobs that offered hazard pay, jobs requiring perfectly legal, non-pornographic performance, jobs as difficult as to be beyond description. Though we dwelt in decaying Hollywood, I always went for day-jobs in expensive upscale business centers. An agency called with an interview for a "discreet secretary with experience handling a medical situation involving changeable behavior." Remove thorn from Godzilla's paw. Ka-ching!

The address belonged to a firm that managed multi-millions of Old Money for trust-fund twits who would otherwise have starved to death. Within the mahogany sanctum, I interviewed with one of the most delightful men I ever met. He possessed a fancy finance degree, combined with a fine sense of humor, immeasurable success in his field and a loving family. He also lived with a life-threatening condition for which no treatment yet existed.

The best available medical advice had given my prospective employer a maximum of five years to live, unless somehow his uniquely volatile blood sugar, fluctuating wildly, instantly and unpredictably, could be stabilized. In order to give his physician the information crucial to his effort to develop a treatment, someone had to get a blood sample from his fingertip while an episode wracked his skeletally thin, frail body and drove his beleaguered brain into angry incoherence.

There was more. The precious drop had to reach the lab for analysis in less than five minutes from acquisition, not a second later. He had established his office in the building where his doctor's lab was located to give this endeavor the best possible chance of success. The whole desperately urgent process had to be accomplished without alerting the clients in the reception area.

This modest, mannerly man gave me permission to do whatever it took to get a blood sample, including twisting his arm, choking him, wrestling him to the floor, and sitting on the middle of his back. He warned me his mood could change in mere seconds and he might throw things at me.

Well, déjà vu, all over again. While my husband had never hit me, he suffered verbally violent outbursts and would strike out against his previous war-time enemies during his frightful nightmares caused by what is now known as PTSD, magnified by the pressure of the tumor on his brain. After describing what was for me routine daily experience, I said I could start the next morning. My desperate employer and several medical collection agencies were thrilled beyond measure.

Each morning began with me sitting in the guest chair in front of my new boss's desk, taking notes on his plan for the day. At any given moment, he would break off mid-sentence, narrow his eyes, and glower at me malevolently. Before he could reach for a heavy object, I would fling the notepad aside, race around the desk with the little device diabetics use, and attempt to prick the end of a finger. Fat chance. There were flailing arms, a twisting torso, and my very real fear of breaking his brittle bones. I tried many times and never succeeded. I was Sisyphus, alas, not Hercules. The pay was great, but eventually, I could not bring myself to keep taking his money. I went job hunting once again.

It is never a failure to try your best and not succeed. The only failure is in not trying.

Metamorphosis

*When opportunity hits you on the head, try
something you've never done before.*

One day I signed up at a temp agency. The next day I emerged a job counselor. I loved that job, because I was making money helping other people get jobs, sometimes even permanent jobs with actual health insurance. I was worshipped as Job Goddess. You can see the attraction.

The experience I gained there convinced another agency to hire me to help open its first California office. We were ensconced in a financial-enclave high-rise, where our prospective clients were principally corporate, banking and real estate law firms. At that glorious time in employment history the law business was booming. Firms competed mightily for the rare secretaries they did not have to train, superwomen who could type 125 wpm with very few errors while withstanding killer 12-15- hour days, relentless deadlines, and the nasty personalities of pressured lawyers. The only attractions of such miserable conditions for legal secretaries were tons of money and health insurance.

After a week at the agency during which our brand-new telephone did not ring once, a law firm called early the next Monday morning. A temp-to-perm legal secretary was needed urgently. This job order was a placement agency's dream: limitless salary depending upon experience; no upper age barrier; and no front-office appearance requirement. Giving preference to numbskull cutie-pies over highly competent plain and/or older women was almost always operative. But in this case, a gorgon who drank at lunch but could still type accurately all afternoon and on into the night, would do just fine. Surely I could find someone.

I naively assured the law firm that I would find someone within the week. Tuesday, Wednesday and Thursday zipped by. I advertised in vain and met with innumerable waiter-guitarists and waitress-actresses. All the while I was stalling the client, assuring the office manager that we would have someone available any moment now. She, in increasingly icy tones, reminded me of my promise. Gulp.

Finally, on fateful Friday morning, I did the only thing I could do to keep my word and hope to retain the client. I sent myself. This was only the agency's second week in business; I was still the only employee. I activated the answering machine, locked the doors, taped up a sign that said "Closed for Family Emergency," and resolutely strode without blindfold toward the firing squad. My reasoning was that, at best, the client had not yet been able to find a secretary anywhere and thus would be grateful if even a warm body showed up. At worst, the office manager, although she did not know my real name, would recognize my voice from our phone conversations, then throw me out and cancel the order. Feeling I had the chance of the proverbial snowball and certain that the agency would fire me in any case, I still saw no other way.

Taking a deep breath and forcing a toothy smile, I breached the doors, and cheerily announced, "The agency sent me." I was sure I had actually screamed out, "I am a complete fake!"

But these harried folks were so busy they would not have noticed if I had. Someone just pointed me toward a desk whereon an IBM electric typewriter and a dictation machine were buried under sloppy piles of line-numbered sheets, which I heard referred to as "pleading paper." Pleading my cause came to mind, but another zombie shoved a cassette in my hand, screeching that whatever was on it was due in court by 4:30. I shoved the tape in the machine, twirled a piece of the mysterious paper around the platen, clapped on the headphones and pretended to understand the barrage of arcane verbiage in my ears. Polishing the garbled grammar as I blazed away, I followed the format I had glimpsed on another document on an adjoining desk.

With the palpitating clumps of my heart in my mouth, I handed my fraudulent final to the office manager. I nearly passed out with relief when she glanced at it, glanced at her watch, didn't glance at my drained face, and sighed, "Thank God! Can you stay late?" Not waiting for my answer, she handed me another blob of words and resumed banging away on her own typewriter. I scurried back to my hole and began feeling as if I might survive, at least until a real legal secretary could be captured. I surreptitiously studied the files for samples of documents resembling whatever I was asked to prepare and began to feel more confident.

However, by the beginning of my second week at the firm, it was obvious to me that there was so much I did not know, I could not maintain my pretense much longer. I wanted to come clean before my cover was blown and get back to base before it was discovered I was AWOL. My conscience had a migraine from the ethics my parents had drilled into my head and the likely possibility that I could make a serious error in ignorance, damaging the firm.

The first moment the office manager and I were alone, I told her the truth. At first she was, justifiably, *really, really, really* angry. Then she offered me the job permanently, telling me she admired my chutzpah. All chutzpah is divided into three parts: gall, guts, and the illogical willingness to take risks against all odds. The office manager figured they could use those qualities around there. The salary she offered me was astronomical compared to my previous pittances. I envisioned hospital bills melting like poet François Villon's "snows of yesteryear" with personal attendants begging to assist my incapacitated husband and debt collectors groveling at my feet.

The catch was, the manager could not afford to wait while I gave the agency proper notice. How to handle this honorably? I made a deal with the agency owner that I would stay at the law firm during the day, thus keeping his client happy, and return to the agency every evening for two weeks for free while he looked for someone to replace me. This worked for everyone.

I was now getting my education as a real legal secretary. I worked with highly experienced women who took the time and trouble to explain things to me at the expense of their own efficiency, a gift I tried to pay forward all my working life. One seasoned secretary in particular knew everything there was to know about the care and feeding of Old Family Money folks, who were the neighbors and social acquaintances of the firm's partners.

While the firm did not technically practice family law, the attorneys quietly handled the internecine domestic wars of people in their set anxious to avoid a public airing of monogrammed dirty linen.

This savvy secretary recalled the time she was filling in at the reception desk when such a man came into the office with a loaded shotgun. He was clearly in search of his divorce-determined wife, meeting there with her attorney. Given that this husband was about to lose at least 50 percent of the family fortune and business, and was facing child support all the way through Ivy League institutions in addition to alimony, it was not hard to envision him slaughtering his wife and everyone else in the office. Which spouse may have been in the right was beside the point.

Knowing the habits and preferences of the local tribe paid off. The secretary calmly greeted the man by his first name, said how nice it was to see him again, and pretended not to notice the shotgun, broken over his Harris-tweeded arm so that the slugs were visible. Saying nothing, he sat down in one of the tapestry wing chairs in the reception area, still holding the gun.

The secretary went into the back room and returned with coffee in delicate Limoges with a sterling teaspoon and two packets of sugar. She intentionally held out the saucered cup in one hand, simultaneously proffering the packets of sugar with the other. The would-be assassin, of course, well-drilled in prep-school manners and dinner party etiquette, had to put down the gun to free both hands in order to take the coffee and the sugar. While he stirred his coffee, our heroine picked up the gun, saying calmly "I'll put this in the closet for you." He stared straight ahead at the wall, sipping his coffee, while she resumed typing at the reception desk, seemingly paying no attention to him. When he had finished the coffee, he politely thanked her and left without asking for his gun.

Fortunately, ours was not a criminal law firm. To the best of my recollection, Harvard Business School statistics in the 1970s listed the average age of death of a criminal defense attorney as 56, by gunshot from a disappointed client, newly released from prison. Family law firm statistics were not far behind.

This was a remarkable act of bravery in an extraordinarily dangerous situation. Absent the secretary's ability to function effectively under great stress, several lives might have ended that day. In ordinary on-the-job situations, make the most of any opportunity to be the employee who manages events, projects and team relationships with calm, rational effectiveness. That will make you very valuable.

"Coffee" Chief 1.0

Risk making a fool of yourself; you may make a success.

"Coffee Chief?" No, a pretense of misunderstanding by a janitor with a sardonic sense of humor. Copy Chief designated my new position at a mail order catalog company. The custodian's joke included cluttering my office with all the lipstick-blotched and cigarette-ash loaded mugs that he picked up around the building every day. It was one of those little attempts at humor we all make to keep ourselves awake, if not sane, on the job.

How and why did I become a Copy Chief? Logic dictated I should have remained in the well-paid legal field where I had already risked making a fool of myself and survived. But all my working life, no matter how good my current job, I regularly looked through the classified ads to see what new opportunities might be available. Having always been a secretary who wrote and edited various things to make the boss look better, I had always dreamed of making a living as a writer under my own name. I had no illusions about writing best-selling novels in a Paris garret. I had to have some kind of salaried job.

One day I spotted an ad for a full-time job writing direct mail advertising copy for a leading company in the field. This was the rare writing job offering a steady salary and health insurance, on solid corporate ground, unlike the tremulous terrain of advertising agencies where your job goes out the door every time a major client slams it. This ad ran continuously for three weeks, telling me no one qualified had applied and/or there was some reason no experienced person wanted the job. If it was that bad, I might get an interview.

"Salary commensurate with experience," threatened the ad. I had no experience: zip, zero, nada. The closest I had ever gotten to direct mail advertising was glancing at unsolicited catalogs of crud on my way to the garbage can. It seemed to me that this was the most simplistic type of writing I had ever seen, involving blurbs of hysteria over wart creme and polyester mumus. Fortunately, I had no idea then of just how difficult this type of writing actually is. Any idiot could write this stuff, I thought.

Corporate writing jobs did not pay as well as legal secretarial jobs. Given my husband's condition, I could never risk putting my income in jeopardy just for personal gratification. I calculated brutal economies for myself until I reached the absolutely rock-bottom figure I could accept without compromising his care. My only ace in the hole was the consistent supply of night-shift legal and medical transcription jobs I could do from home. These were always available for the usual reason: very few qualified secretaries needed or wanted them.

Keeping the new job as Copy Chief for Chatchkes and Cheap Crap, Inc. proved to be easy, but applying for it had been tricky, demanding an unorthodox approach. I had to apply for the job in such a manner as to show that while I had no experience, I had sufficient ability. My best hope was that the company was desperate. I called and was granted an interview.

Now I had to invent some sort of portfolio to show my "work." I fished a couple of catalogs out of the trash, cut them up and mounted on cardboard some ads for typical products such as overnight skin rejuvenators, miracle weight-loss pills and gigantic vinyl tote bags. I renamed the products and wrote descriptions I felt would win more buyers than the professional copy currently used. I juxtaposed my versions with the original copy and sallied forth, my pathetic paste-ups in my briefcase and my heart in my mouth.

Upon arrival, I was taken to a huge conference table where several executives and the Art Director waited in stony silence. They murmured among themselves over my fakes, never addressing me personally. Finally I was handed a sample jar of a facelift formula, a concoction of glycerin, rosewater, and something temporarily tightening that would allow customers to appear younger for a guaranteed millisecond. They asked me to take this product home, ponder its virtues, and then describe them appealingly within a very tight word limit. While nothing was said directly, they made it clear I was to stay just within the letter of the law defining what could be claimed without resulting in a lawsuit for false advertising.

I took in this new and startling information with as bland an expression as I could maintain and responded that I would be glad to write the ad right there. This brash, risky ploy was impressive for more reasons than I realized at the time. The mail order catalog business, I soon learned, requires rapid copy composition and constant on-the-spot edits to adjust page space for product photos that often turn out to be larger or smaller than planned. Some products are replaced at the last minute. Thus the copy chief must instantly produce a description in final form, while the press starts rolling.

I transmuted the greasy gunk into "Pink Pearlescence." I extolled the product as giving the "feeling" of youthfulness and stated that a single jar would last next to eternity "if used as recommended." Continuing, I proclaimed that the buyer could have a "whole new outlook on life" for a mere pittance and ended with the warning that she should order right away because this was a "limited edition." I asked for the use of a typewriter and churned out a double-spaced final. I left the building confident I had aced the test.

The very next morning, I got a phone call asking me to come in for a second interview. Mr. Manager said, "It's obvious you are very talented, but equally obvious you have no experience." I reiterated that I had truthfully stated outright when I first came in that I had no experience in this field but was willing to learn. I was prepared to be thanked for my time and propelled out the door, feeling like a fool. After all, when you put your head in the lion's mouth, you should expect it to be bitten off, right?

Instead, Mr. Manager said because I would have to learn some aspects of the business on the job, the salary would be less than it would have been for someone with experience. That's when I realized he was actually offering me the job. Yes, I said gravely, I would expect that. We agreed on a start date, and I left elated, but also feeling as disconcerted as a vampire whose coffin suddenly opened in the sun.

Once on the job, I soon realized that this outfit had been up against the wall with dangerous publishing deadlines, was not offering nearly enough money at best to entice a professional, and would have hired the devil if he'd promised not to scorch the pages. Foregoing some income and job security were the price of entrée into the world of daytime wordsmithing. I wanted to find out once and for all if I could succeed in that realm, so I decided to tough it out on short money until I could gain sufficient experience and industry knowledge to improve the dollars, there or with the competition.

Oh, yes, they used my Pink Pearlescence copy. One customer ate a whole jar of it. She wrote that she figured a large amount would work better than a small one and work even better from the inside than the outside. She further advised me that while she had not yet noticed a reduction in wrinkles, she had experienced a salutary laxative effect.

Think very hard before you give up what you've got for something else. If it means enough to you, get a foot in the door, prove your worth and make yourself ready to move up.

Copy Chief 2.1

Hard-Won Experience Pays Off.

My "coffee chief" job gave me a rare look behind the scenes in the very complicated mail order business. When I finished cutting my baby teeth there, I grew fangs. Now I was armed with copy-writing experience and had a track record of performing on schedule under intense deadline pressure regardless of the potholes in the path to print. I was ready to market myself for more money.

My opportunity came when a copy chief at the direct mail division of a national corporate kingdom found the guts to make the leap into an advertising agency. I had no such courage and could not have afforded to take the risk if I had; he had a working wife, I had a sick husband. It was enough for me that I could at least now present my seasoned self as a candidate to replace him. Fortunately, effective direct mail copy hacks with managerial abilities were rare. I was hired on the basis of my experience, without an interview, via a single brief, static-disrupted phone conversation. The deadline-driven voice on the line asked how much and when. I said "lots" and "two weeks." Done deal.

With this position came with a glass cube where I would spend my long days and nights, a staff of two copywriters, 1/5 of a fragmented secretary and a whole new world of multi-tasking. I had to write and edit on the hoof and coordinate my department's efforts with photography, layout and print production.

There were two layers of management above my barely middle-managerial head. This meant I could neither hire nor fire. Alcohol on the job was the norm in corporate advertising departments in those years, as well as in agencies, as I hope you have seen brilliantly and accurately depicted on the TV series Mad Men. Several people in my department, from top management to lowly drudge, took turns staying sober in rotation so that one of them could always cover for the rest. My only libation was French roast, thus I was not popular. However, they all knew they could count on me to handle business every day. This set my job security in cement.

It helps if you're popular, but if your skills are good enough, that's enough. Being able to function independently when others are dysfunctional gives you an edge. Your job security increases when others rely on you.

Copy Chief 2.2

Help Someone Else and You Will Always Help Yourself, Too.

One day we had an opening for a copywriter. It was my task to solicit résumés, interview the likely candidates, and then present the finalist to the two Higher-Ups to whom I reported for their decision. Everybody wants to be a writer and many who could would never get the chance owing to someone screening for extensive direct experience. Translation: the company did not want to spend time and money training an inexperienced person if it could hire a seasoned professional, accustomed to grinding out perfect prose under unceasingly brutal deadline pressure. Burned in my memory was my amateurish presentation of sample copy for the coffee chief job, which I had gotten at least partially because someone took a chance on me. I knew I was quite likely throwing away a worthy person every time I tossed a résumé on the reject pyre.

Our ad generated nearly 300 hopefuls, including an Ivy League screenwriting student, several unpublished novelists, a single mother who had written a classified ad to sell her sofa to feed her kids, and many people who wrote insurance policies (as Joseph Heller did to eat while he wrote Catch 22). I winnowed the crop to 15 folks with heavy agency and/or corporate advertising writing experience, knowing my masters would never consider any of the others. With the cruelest of blades, I pared this group down to 5. I met with 4, any of whom could have done the job.

This left one, who stood far above the rest. Matchless in direct experience and multi-talented, she was an enigma wrapped in a mystery. Her résumé showed no address or telephone number. Not only had she 20 years of direct mail and agency copy-writing and editing experience, she was also an equally experienced layout artist and pre-print production manager. She was the whole package, someone who could do her job, my job, and several other people's jobs, competently cover for absences and flexibly fill in wherever we needed her most. Her resume showed no address or telephone number. How to reach her?

Just then, she called me from a phone booth near where she was living in her car with her cat. This she stated without explanation in a pleasant, calm drawl. She would like to come in with her portfolio before her last clean outfit got dirty. Also, if I did not want to hire her, she needed to know right away so that she could get another job before her cat ran out of food and fresh litter. She made no mention of needing food herself. I knew instantly she was the person I wanted, but that I would have to repackage her to make her palatable to the decision-makers. I said, "Please come in." She said it would take her about 20 minutes to make it, walking.

She entered my office clean and neat. How she managed that, camping in her car, I could not imagine. She sat reading one of our catalogs while I looked at her portfolio. I would never be as valuable in the business as she was; I should have been working for her. I explained I had no authority to hire and asked to keep her portfolio overnight so that I could present it to the High Hierarchy the next morning. She stood up, thanked me, shook my hand, and said she would call me tomorrow about noon.

Now I really had to write some convincing copy. I retyped her résumé to list the address and phone number of a friend of mine, whom I could bribe with dinner to say this stranger was her roommate. It was too late by then to check references in distant time zones, but I knew I didn't need to do that anyway. Next morning I whipped into the office of the Copy King, courageously interrupted his final proofing sign-off of a deadline job, and slid her résumé and portfolio under his nose. This was a guy with more years in the business than I had then been alive, dour, humorless, and forbidding. Also, he didn't like me. I was positive he had thought when he hired me via our bad-connection telephone call that "Dana" was a man. So disappointing! He glanced at her résumé and the first two pages of the portfolio, shutting it smartly and returning to the proofing job without ever looking up at me across the desk. My heart sank as I got up to leave, but suddenly he said: "I have to show this to the Art Director; see me tomorrow." That gave me hope, but time was running out. Tomorrow had to be as distant as eternity to this woman and her cat.

She called me at noon precisely. I told her the chances were good that the Copy King would not bother to discuss her work with the Art Emperor if he were not interested, but I could not guarantee anything. She said, "I understand your position, but I can only call you one more time, because the next dime is the last dime." I promised to let her know by 4. She said she'd call. I made it through the afternoon with antacid tablets and one eye on my watch. As of 3:50 p.m., I had still heard nothing from Big Art. Having little to lose, I poked my head into his lair and said as casually as I could muster: "So, whad'ja think?" Without lifting his drawing pen from the page or looking up, déjà never-viewed as I always was, he asked, "So when can she start?" Ah, deadly deadlines, ever my allies, to the rescue. I said that, very fortunately for us, although she was in high demand, she happened to be available tomorrow. I then blazed toward my office, where the phone was ringing. I grabbed it and bellowed, "You got it!" Placid as a pond, she said, "Good, I'll be there at 8 tomorrow." Thus began one of the finest professional relationships of which I have ever had the pleasure of being a part.

*Help everyone you can. It will help you
more than you can imagine.*

The Ironic Health Insurance Company Job

Take a job with real benefits and leave when they're not.

By 1975 my husband's condition was dire. Having proven to myself that I could cut it as a writer of something made it less painful to accept the necessity to return to the realm of highly-paid secretaries and attendant oodles of overtime. At least I wasn't leaving because I had failed. On my way to law firm interviews, I stumbled across a secretarial job at an insurance company with a dream benefit, a health plan that actually covered dependents without any exclusionary provisions. A miracle! But first, we had to survive the three-month waiting period.

Holding my breath, I checked off the days on my desk calendar. We almost made it. Exactly 12 hours before the expiration of the three-month period, my husband collapsed.

He was disoriented in the extreme and his vision in the remaining sighted eye was almost gone. I rushed him to the office of an ophthalmic surgeon we knew only slightly, having nowhere else to turn. Examining my husband immediately, the doctor, although unable to see the tumor, concluded there had to be something pressing on the optic nerve, that it could only be a tumor, and that there was not a moment to lose. A true humanitarian, knowing we had no money or insurance, this physician drove my husband to the hospital, by-passed the check-in procedure and wheeled him directly into the newly invented brain scanner. This courageous physician risked his license to practice and the withdrawal of his operating privileges to do this.

A mass about the size of a walnut was at last visible. By great good fortune, the chief neurosurgeon was currently the director of the hospital and a man with ethics to match those of the ophthalmologist. He operated immediately, with no questions asked, successfully removing the tumor. This saved my husband's life, greatly relieved his pain and restored his vision to a considerable degree, but most of the damage was not reversible.

Naturally, the insurance megalith refused my desperate, tearful pleading to waive the 12 hours. What was I thinking?! No person that sick and expensive could ever be allowed coverage. That was not the way insurance companies got rich. Stupid me!

I owed $140,000 to the hospital, whose chief finance officer was poised to garnishee my salary, my husband's last line of defense. I beat the CFO to the punch with bankruptcy. I then had to find a way to convince the hospital to allow my husband crucial post-surgical follow-up procedures, the right to which I had just forfeited. I offered the astonished CFO a deal in which I would voluntarily pay the entire bill, but in small, regular payments, even though the hospital could not now collect a penny from me, in exchange for any continuing care ordered by the surgeons. The CFO convinced the hospital board of directors that something was better than nothing. His proviso was that if I ever missed a single payment, my husband was out.

Unlike the hospital, the neurosurgical team and back-up team members, 10 in all, generously wrote off one-half their fees and accepted small monthly payments for the rest for eternity without making me grovel. While this was benevolence beyond belief, I still owed them $170,000.

Time to leave the loathsome insurance company and get another job, one with an endless supply of overtime.

Don't let a setback stop you.

Foreign Affairs Factotum

*Skills you never thought you'd use may
be the ones you need the most.*

M Y HUSBAND WAS finally well enough to be moved and I desperately needed a change of scene. The debt would follow me wherever I went, of course. My record of faithful payments to the hospital and the neurosurgeons would provide the references to convince new hospitals, doctors and caregivers to trust me, so that my husband's care would continue wherever we went. My hard-working aunt inspired me to move to San Francisco, city of my youthful dreams, saying: "If you have to work like a dog and can't afford to travel, at least live where you would like to be on vacation." Woof.

Upon arrival, I rented a dump, left my husband in the safest hands I could afford and hot-footed it to the nearest large law firm, one step ahead of the next medical installment.

For several years, I had had to hide my BA because it made me "overqualified" for secretarial jobs, so I showed only my high school education on my résumé. Further, I dared not state that I could take briefhand dictation. A secretary who could take dictation was in a higher salary category than a "typist" who transcribed taped dictation. Employers didn't want to pay for hand-taken dictation if they could avoid it. Thus, I was a usually hired as a typist and my briefhand dictation speed of the standard 70 words per minute, mothballed since college note taking, had slipped to about 45 words per minute.

Thus reduced, I was stunned to discover my interviewer was considering only those secretarial applicants with at least a BA and hand-dictation of no less than 70 words per minute. Fortunate beyond belief, I had thrown my framed degree in my tote bag when we moved and forgotten to take it out. As to dictation, sure, I lied. I was told I would be called for a second interview in about a week.

Now I had to figure out how to get up to speed quickly. Racing home, I scanned radio stations for a speaker who droned at minimally 70 words per minute. I hit paydirt with a leather-lungs preacher who raved hellfire and brimstone throughout a non-stop three hour daily broadcast at a steady 75. After four days I had a thorough understanding of where I would spend eternity if I failed to send a check and could rip through 75+ in my sleep. I was ready when I got the call.

Once on-board, I discovered that a senior partner had represented the USA in high-level post-WWII European negotiations. His firm specialized in international clients. Among them the principal language of business, finance, law and diplomatic-level dinner parties was still French. Upon learning that the firm needed someone to take notes and make civilized conversation at client meetings, I thought I could now mention that, oh, by the way, I was a fairly good francophone and could also manage basic Spanish.

The partner engaged me in a test conversation in French, whereupon I was able to name drop advantageously. For a brief Warholian 15 minutes of fame years before, I interpreted for the former Premier of France, Pierre Mendès-France, Ph.D. in Economics, during his lecture tour in Portland, Oregon. Dr. Mendès-France did not need an interpreter, but nonetheless I had the job and the official title, thanks to a generous language professor who had bravely gone to bat for me. The partner had worked with Dr. Mendès-France in Europe. Bingo! I was the new International Secretary. Terrific title upgrade, same old salary. You can't win 'em all.

Continuing at the firm I used some French every day, but it appeared after many months there would be no occasion to use Spanish. However, one night when I was working overtime, a newly minted attorney suddenly started racing around the floor, screaming frantically: "Does anyone speak Spanish?!" I was the only other human being left in the office except the janitor, a former engineer, fluent in Mandarin and German.

I couldn't imagine why there would be an urgent need for Spanish at 9. The hyperventilating tyro explained that one of his assignments had been to move to the U.S. several hundred thousand dollars of a client's money then reposing in a South American country's bank. The controlling political party, having just staged a successful coup, was going to nationalize the bank at midnight our time. Read: grab all the money. The leader of the party, naturally also the director of the bank, was anxious not to offend trading partners. To this end, he had given foreign clients and their lawyers a few days' notice to remove funds.

The exhausted, worked-to-death new lawyer charged with arranging the transfer had forgotten to do it until this moment. His career would be over at the stroke of midnight unless he could reach the bank and convince the revolutionary government to wire-transfer the money to our client's U.S. bank.

In the face of his desperation, I said I would try. Handing me the South American bank's telephone number and the client's U.S. bank's transfer code, he collapsed into a chair with his head in his hands.

By now, it was 9:15. The international operator tried the number. Minutes went by with incessant ringing through 9:25. Suddenly, with a crackling burst of static, there came on the line a faint voice demanding "Who is this?!" in something far from the literary Spanish my juvenile self had read in Cervantes. I could hear men shouting at each other in the background. We had reached a soldier on a field telephone somewhere around the capital.

I launched into my spiel, which went something like: "This is the law firm of blah, blah calling for the Most Distinguished Director of the Bank." The soldier responded with the equivalent of "Huh?" and the line went dead. I made the call again, flying through 9:50, the attorney turning pale, breathing shallowly. I finally reached another private in another outpost, repeated the above speech and at last was transferred to a sergeant. I made the speech again and again as the line repeatedly died and revived. The clock whizzed by 10:30. The attorney's eyes were now glazed; he mumbled incoherently about methods of suicide and having wasted parental money on a fine law school.

After many more agonizing minutes there was at last a clear connection to a voice speaking much more polished Spanish, Officer Something. By now, my highly practiced speech was glibly rolling in fake fluency. I hoped I was conveying the impression I was secretary to an influential big-wig U.S. Lawyer and hoped His Excellency would deign—grovel, scrape—to speak with me. I held my breath while the voice paused to weigh the possibility of offending an important U.S. entity against the danger of disturbing The President with something unwelcome.

After what seemed an eternity, the voice politely asked if I would kindly wait just a moment, please. You bet I would. The moment was now 11:50. Hoping against hope that The President would somehow actually come on the phone, I readied the most formal, respectful sentence my limited Spanish would allow, worrying that if I did get him, he would insist on speaking to another man. Suddenly, the smooth official voice of a minion handing the telephone to Someone said in lyrical Spanish: "Mr. President, it is a lady from a U.S. law firm." I readied my only weapon, took a deep breath, and was struck dumb. The voice said in the finest Eton-through-Oxford English : "Good evening. This is The President. How may I assist you, Madam?"

Eyes riveted on 11:55, I jerked into English, explaining how very sorry we were to trouble his august self at this very busy and important juncture in his country's history. With pure invention, I explained that our unfortunate client, one of our smaller, charity-case pro bono types, to whose survival even the paltry sum in question was crucial, had somehow naively overlooked the deadline. Would he therefore kindly transfer their funds to their U.S. bank in a gracious gesture of international cooperation? Without a pause, the President said: "Why certainly, Madam, it would be my pleasure. I shall just wire transfer now." I gave him the code, he gave the instruction, and the clock gave us midnight.

I thanked him profusely for his benevolence, extended so graciously. He reminisced longingly about how much he missed his student days in England and how he hoped to visit New York and attend the Metropolitan Opera. He eventually signed off with a cheery "Righty ho," and so ended the crisis.

The young attorney revived with an injection of black-sludge coffee and the prospect of life after near-death. The client was in reality one so powerful it would have wrung from the firm every penny of the lost funds plus the maximum millions winnable under our malpractice coverage. The resulting publicity would likely have caused The Firm to lose all the rest of its clients, not merely this one. The young attorney would never have worked again, as long as he lived, even as a rag picker. As it was, no one was harmed and I made some extra overtime money.

This is important enough to say again: never let even the least of your skills slide. You may be able to do something no one else can do. You don't have to be perfect to be effective.

Networking Nets a Great Job

*The person who appears least likely may
be the very one you need the most.*

For example, I was working as a corporate litigation secretary when I met a temp soon to be full-time at another firm nearby. Our entire acquaintance consisted of a single 10-minute coffee break conversation. During that time, we discovered we shared the same outrageous, socially unacceptable, politically incorrect sense of humor. That brief connection went: hello, witty comments, big laughter, exchange of phone numbers, good bye and good luck.

A few days later, the medical community let me know I needed a better job. I planned to dedicate an entire precious lunch hour, which commodity I normally sold for overtime, to phoning everyone on my Rolodex, that early data storage unit, hoping someone knew of an opening. By serendipitous fortune, I bumped the Rolodex with my coffee mug. It fell open to the temp's name, located about half-way between A and Z. Although I would have called her in due alphabetical course, I thought she was the very least likely person in my entire collection of job contacts to want or be able to help me. After all, she barely knew me, had no clues about my skills other than knowing I could do whatever I did there well enough to have kept the job for a few years, and was probably very busy handling her own new job. I only called her first because her name and number chanced to flop in front of my face.

I got to"Hi, it's me…" when she barked into the phone: "Get over here now! The one they hired just bailed. You're the perfect person for this job!"

"What is it?" I asked.

"Biotech Patent Secretary," she said.

"Never heard of it," said the ignoramus.

"They never heard of you either," she replied. " Just get over here!"

I learned that highly specialized biotech patent secretaries were hard to come by. At my interview I learned the firm had made an offer to the only qualified candidate who had responded to either their ad or their agency request. She was the ideal patent secretary, highly experienced and acknowledged in the field as able to do the complex work involved blindfolded. At the last minute, she opted for the larger firm down the street, unable to refuse its counter-offer of much more money than the smaller firm could afford to pay. While the larger firm's salary was stratospherically high, the smaller firm's was still higher than I had ever been offered.

When I interviewed I imagined there were many other eager applicants panting for this extremely well-paid job. I had no idea just how difficult and demanding this specialized legal work actually was. Thus, when the firm hired me, I puffed up with pride like a blowfish, figuring that in some way I just had to be much better than the rest. Fishing for a compliment, I inquired of my new boss: "Why did you hire me? " He said "No one else wanted the job." Definitely not flattering, but as I said before, definitely a guaranteed way to get hired.

This generous patent attorney took the time and trouble to teach me how to be a patent secretary, with which skill I earned an unusually good living for the remaining years of my working life. I treasure his comment, made after we had worked together several years: "I wouldn't be nearly as successful as I am if you didn't work for me." He and his wife, also a respected patent professional, remain my dear friends to this day.

I stayed there as long as he did, then was able to use what he taught me to get a much more highly paid patent secretarial job elsewhere. Of greatest satisfaction to me is that, over my 28 years as a patent secretary, I was able to pay his gift forward. Of the 10 people I trained, some of whom had no legal secretarial experience at all, nine make an excellent living as patent secretaries and paralegals. If I needed a job now, I guarantee that each one of them would fight for me.

Network, network, network! Burn up the internet. Don't throw anyone away. Never presume a contact is trivial.

Odd Jobs

Keep a record of people's names, what kind of work they do and where to reach them. Maintain contact often enough to keep the information current. Make sure they remember your name and how to reach you. Always send a hand-written thank-you note for an interview.

Midnight Mail Madness

*Apply for jobs with consistent overtime
no one else wants to work.*

IN 1991 I was able to combine resources with another woman in a tough position. My husband and I moved into her home, renting the top floor. The rent money she got from me kept her from losing her home. In turn I got a nice place to live and a safe place to keep my husband with her help to watch over him. My salary and overtime as a biotech patent secretary carried the three of us through his death in 2007 and hers in 2010. You, too, may be able to make an arrangement like this to help yourself and someone else.

I kept the biotech patent secretarial job from the 1990s until retirement in 2011. To understand why I was paid so much money and what I had to do to earn it requires a little background information. A principal goal of a patent firm is to somehow get its client's patent application to the

United States Patent and Trademark Office (USPTO) before another firm can do that with its client's patent application on an arguably identical invention. If Firm A fails to do this, the dreaded precedence of the Firm B's client's invention is established, dashing Firm A's client's hopes of making money on its invention. The clients are pharmaceutical, computing and industrial giants with research connected to major universities and government entities worldwide. Billions of bucks, not mere millions, are at stake.

An additional deadline responsibility occurs whenever a client advises that one of its employee-inventors is scheduled to speak at a scientific conference on a given day.

Any patent application relevant to the invention upon which the inventor is planning to discourse must reach the USPTO by midnight of the day before the inventor gets on the plane. It is understandable that an exuberant inventor whose research has just been funded might excitedly tell convivial colleagues at the hotel bar all about it the evening before the formal presentation. Such alcohol-induced public disclosure of the information renders it public property, no longer private, patentable, profitable intellectual property.

When I started this job, computer wizardry had not yet bestowed upon us the ability to electronically transmit time-sensitive patent applications to the USPTO. East Coast patent firms, with the filing deadline of midnight, had the advantage over West Coast firms by virtue of location. In order to level the playing field, the USPTO considered West Coast patent applications sent by Express Mail to be filed timely if the Express Mail package was time-stamped at the local post office before midnight of a given day.

Nonetheless we propitiated a harsh deity. We had up to one nanosecond before midnight to reach the post office and obtain a receipt, proving we had lain our Express Mail packages on the altar within the time limit. Upon this fragile scrap of paper everything depended. I coined overtime regularly helping prepare deadline applications and their accompanying government forms, then delivering them to the post office by cab, almost always five nights per week for eight years.

It often took us until very close to midnight to finish the requisite paperwork. Only one postal station in the entire Bay Area was open that late, the Airport Post Office (APO) in South San Francisco, far from the financial district where we slaved. The APO is technically located a mere 14.2 miles and 22 minutes down the freeway as the crow flies. The reality was that the cab, at top speed, had to run the gamut of constant late-night road maintenance, detours, overturned 18-wheelers, wet weather, and hungry highway patrol officers trolling for scofflaws like us. The APO building, eternally under reconstruction, lurked in a swampy field off an unmarked, unpaved, unlit mud track sunk deep within the morass of the airport cargo area. Cabs often could not get through as far as the asphalt parking lot; I frequently had to hoof it by flashlight quite a bit of the way.

To make matters worse, all of us bedraggled night shifters had usually endured a grueling 12-hour day before the evening's marathon began. Envision exhausted lawyers scrivening frantically to translate scientists' scribbled notes into the arcane patois spoken by the USPTO as the clock advances mercilessly. We had to deal with inventors' last-minute changes, jammed copiers, clogged staplers, power failures, and blurry faxes obscuring vital experimental results. The final straw came when our then state-of-the-art computer programs crashed under the demands of complex chemical patent drawings. Sometimes an attorney had to patch these up by hand, under a wavering flashlight beam, in a cab rocketing toward the post office.

I had to invent ways to stay alert enough not to make a fatal error in my part of the paperwork. My best allies were hunger and the icy temperature of the office tower after the heat shut down at 5.

I also found it useful to flop down onto the dirty carpet with my feet higher than my head for a few minutes every couple of hours. Absent a hot meal and a warm sweater to lull me into deadly lethargy, and with a blast of blood to my flagging brain, I stayed sharp enough to survive the ordeal. Remember, there is always a way. You may not like the way, but there is always a way.

Now, the agonies of preparation are at last over and the Express Mail package is in my hands. It's about 11 on a good night and about 11:30 on a bad one. Worst of all nights it was 17 minutes, 30 seconds to 12…My task was always to blaze out of the tower, race across the plaza, fling myself into a waiting cab, barrel down the freeway and reach the APO in time to scramble through the automatically closing double-doors, behemoths of steel-rimmed glass, before they met on either side of my face.

In order to give myself the best possible chance of a successful journey, I booked cabs days in advance, with regular drivers who knew exactly where the APO was, what the difficulties and dangers of the journey were, and that they would be tipped handsomely for taking serious risks involving highest possible speed and tickets on their record. The drivers earned enough to send their kids to Harvard. The firm offered to pay the tickets and I carried a million dollar life insurance policy in my husband's favor.

I instituted the policy of a back-up cab to follow my cab in case it was nabbed for speeding. My idea was to jump into the second cab and hope to make the APO before that cab was caught. Worst-case scenario, I would stay with my cab driver, if the highway patrol insisted, and toss the package to the driver of the back-up cab, who would blaze toward the APO and take the package in himself. If he got pulled over, all would be lost.

At last my cab is careening down the freeway. We screech to a halt at the construction barrier around the bog surrounding the APO like a moat. I turn on my flashlight, clutch the package in a vise-like grip, and enter the forest primeval. I slog my way across partially downed fences, over ditches, and through the weedy swamp to the parking lot in front of the building. I squish up the stairs, slipping in mud and slime, defying the massive doors grinding toward me. Deadline met.

One night there was the added obstacle of a mismarked construction detour that put the cab driver and me directly in the path of incoming Coast Guard helicopters. As the landing strip lights came up, a security guard burst out of a hut and screamed: "Incoming aircraft! Get out of here!" We did. The driver patched out and I jumped out, landing in a brush pile through which the faint lights of the APO could be glimpsed. Neither sleet nor snow nor incoming aircraft shall ...

By far the most spectacular deadline-save in my experience of this strange job occurred the night the package did not reach the street outside our building until the aforementioned 17 minutes, 30 seconds to midnight. Both cabs I had booked in advance for the run had been suddenly commandeered for visiting Washington, DC dignitaries, leaving us cabless and terrified. We were amazed to discover that the wife of one of the waylaid cab drivers, summoned by her husband, was idling at the curb in her rusty old Toyota Corolla, ready to drive me. The attorney for whom I was working that night, gentleman that he was, had accompanied me outside. He was loathe to let me take the risk of whatever top speed could be gotten out of such dubious and unauthorized transport and thus hopped in with the package himself. The moment they took off, I was by chance able to grab a cab and blaze after them.

Mrs. Cab Driver and her beater Toyota proved themselves worthy of the Daytona 500 and the Paris-Dakar. She made a screaming turn into the APO parking lot with 30 seconds to spare. The attorney, fortunately young, agile, thin, and possessed of very long legs, made a leap worthy of the Bolshoi though the slender space remaining between the Jaws of Death, which snapped shut behind his coattail. The awestruck clerks burst into cheers and I, being right behind him outside the glass, thought I should alert the San Francisco Ballet to its next premier danseur.

This bizarre overtime stint paid the majority of my husband's remaining massive bills and carried him through comfortably to his death in 2007. While he at last became insurable to a degree in the 1990s, the past financial damage was so great that coverage was virtually irrelevant. Without this extra income, my regular salary, although very generous, would never have been enough. Many families still have it far worse than we did. As this is written, President Obama is trying to change that.

Look for a vital function nobody else wants to perform and offer to take responsibility for it. Prove your dependability; let the employer see that you can be counted on absolutely. That may prove more important than any skill you have. I was never the best or the smartest employee, but I was always the most reliable.

What Now?

This book won't save you and neither will any other book. Only you can do that. Don't give up. There is always a way. You may not like the way, but there is always a way.

Please let me know when you find yours at Dana.Grae.Kane@gmail.com.

CPSIA information can be obtained at www.ICGtesting.com
Printed in the USA
BVOW09s1618250214

345969BV00001B/9/P